The Raft Race

Written by Roderick Hunt
Illustrated by Alex Brychta

OXFORD
UNIVERSITY PRESS

The children were at the river.

It was raft race day.

Mum and Dad made a raft.

The children helped.

"This is a good raft," said Dad.
"Let's get it into the water."

They slid the raft into the water.
Dad pulled it. Wilma and Chip
pushed.

Mum and Dad got on.

"Don't fall in," said Wilf.

The raft race started. Mum and
Dad went fast.

"Go! Go! Go!" shouted Biff.
"You can win."

Mum and Dad went faster.
"Come on!" puffed Dad. "We
can win."

Oh no! The raft broke.

SPLASH! Dad fell in the water.

"Go on, Mum," shouted Wilf.

"You can still win."

Mum kept going.

Dad got back on his raft.

"Go on, Dad," shouted Wilma.

"Go as fast as you can."

Oh no! The raft broke again.

SPLASH! Dad fell in the water.

Mum kept going and she
won the race!

"Good old Mum," said Wilma.

"Poor old Dad," said Wilf.

Talk about the story

Why did the raft break in half?

What did Dad do after the raft broke?

The children were pleased for Mum. How did they feel about Dad?

Have you ever been in a boat or on a raft? What would you do if you fell in?

Find the pairs

Each set of creatures has an odd one out.
Can you find each one?

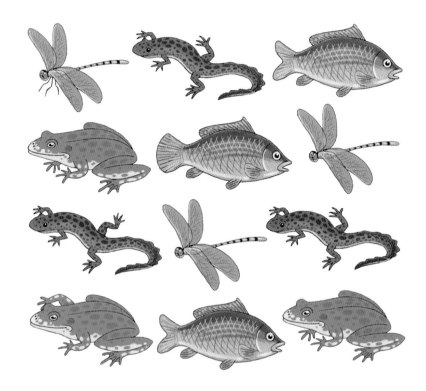